BRINGING UP A PUPPY

Esther Verhoef

BRINGING UP A PUPPY

REBO
PUBLISHERS

© 1998 Zuid Boekprodukties
© 2006 Rebo Publishers

Text and photographs: Esther Verhoef
Cover design and layout: Mesika Design, Hilversum, The Netherlands
Typesetting and pre-press services: A. R. Garamond, Prague,
The Czech Republic
Americanization: Andrew Mikolajski for First Edition Translations Ltd,
Cambridge, UK
Proofreading: Sarah Dunham

ISBN 13: 978-90-366-1556-3
ISBN 10: 90-366-1556-9

CONTENTS

1 WHO IS THE BOSS?

The pack

To bring up and look after a puppy well, it is necessary to know as much as possible about its needs, motives, and body language. This knowledge can be applied to the mutual benefit of you and your dog.

The dog's behavior can easily be compared to that of the wolf.

The white poodle clearly feels that it is the strongest of the bunch

Wolves live in packs. Because of their numbers and perfect teamwork, they can get the better of prey which is much larger and stronger than themselves, and can confront their most dangerous opponents. This way of life requires great social bonding in the pack. It also depends on just one wolf leading the group. At the head of every pack of wolves is the alpha-wolf. This is usually a male. The second in rank is the beta-wolf. The lowest in rank is the omega-wolf.

Rank and class

The alpha-wolf is the leader of the pack. This is the most intelligent, the strongest, and also the most dominant wolf. The alpha has privileges which no other wolf has. For example, the alpha is the first to eat and is allowed to lie, sit, and walk just as it sees fit. The others stand aside for it. It may also correct (bite) a subordinate that takes liberties. In return, the alpha-wolf shows the other members of the pack where the prey lies and chooses, for example, the ideal moment for the hunt. The

Right: Pack-forming is of vital importance to wolves

beta-wolf has all the privileges which the alpha-wolf has, but only with respect to the wolves that are lower in rank. The beta-wolf behaves toward the alpha-wolf just like all the others—respectfully. The third in rank only needs to consider the alpha- and the beta-wolf and so it continues until we reach the omega-wolf. This one can be snarled at by everybody and gets the last scraps of food. This seems hard but, in spite of its low rank, it is advantageous to belong to the group. For its food and safety it is dependent on the skills of the animals above it. In addition to this, those lower in rank have an important task to fulfill. When the most senior in rank go hunting, the lowest stay behind in the camp to sound the alarm if anything happens. The penetrating howl reaches the pack miles away and will urge them to return to the camp.

Respect
As a rule, wolves have a solemn respect for higher-ranking ani-

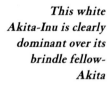

This white Akita-Inu is clearly dominant over its brindle fellow-Akita

The body language of the wolf is comparable to that of our dog

mals. No wolf would ever dream of stealing food from under the nose of a higher-ranked wolf or of crossing him or her in any way. Wolves which take liberties are corrected hard and directly by the higher-ranking wolves. Only if the leader, through age or illness, makes mistakes, thus endangering the further existence of the pack, will his position of power be challenged. From the ensuing fight it becomes clear which is the stronger. If it proves to be the young male, then from that moment on he is the pack's new leader.

Body language
Because wolves really need each other, they prefer not to fight among themselves. Only if the leader is an incompetent pack leader, or a disturbed wolf whose deviant behavior causes problems, does it come to a scrap. This only happens, however, when the continued existence of the pack is in danger. In all other cases, wolves usually display body language to make things clear to each other. Thus a more senior wolf will show its rank during a confrontation with a pack member who is lower in rank by carrying its tail high, ears pricked, and head as high as possible. It literally shows its higher rank. The other

With its body held low and ears folded back, this puppy is showing that it is lower in rank

Right: This dog will certainly let fly if the Weimaraner does not leave it alone

shows by its lower bearing that it is in agreement with the division of roles. So during a confrontation such as this the subordinate carries its tail very low or between its legs, its ears are back, and it has a somewhat low-profile attitude. If the senior wolf looks directly at the subordinate, the latter will react by averting its eyes and often turn its head away. Sometimes the senior in rank lays its head on the head, back, or neck of the subordinate. The subordinate then reacts by licking the chin of the senior wolf. Pups do this to get their mother to regurgitate some pre-digested food for them, and subordinate animals do it to show higher-ranked animals that they really are lower in rank.

In a serious confrontation, the subordinate turns on to its back with its belly and neck toward the higher in rank. These parts of the body are very vulnerable and, even though the higher in rank could now seriously injure its opponent, it will not do this. Displaying the belly thus greatly reduces aggression in wolves. No emotionally-sound wolf would bite another member of the pack in such a position of surrender.

Domestication

You will certainly recognize in your pup a number of postures seen in wolves. It too puts its tail between its legs and licks you under the chin. The behavior patterns of our domestic dog can often be traced to the behavior that we know in wolves. However, in the course of that domestication process, which has taken thousands of years, some differences have occurred. This is because, over the centuries, dogs have been selected by man for certain characteristics. The wolf would rather flee than pick a fight with a fierce and able-bodied quarry, but terriers and other breeds which have specifically been bred to overpower or kill game look for confrontation and enjoy it too! So, the self-preservation instinct is less-developed in most domesticated dogs than in the wolf. The gesture of submission which strongly inhibits aggression in wolves is not always mutually understood by dogs. A number of behavioral patterns have thus been lost in the course of time but there are still enough comparable examples of behavior remaining, so that by studying wolf behavior we can also understand the motives of our domestic dog better.

Wolf versus dog

The wolf lives in a pack, your dog lives in your family. For your dog, the family is the pack. It feels safe and happy in a family where the balance of power and the limits of permissible

Dogs are pack animals, just like wolves

*The future
character can often
be seen at a young
age*

behavior are clear. The family has a pack leader too and it does not matter whether this is a man or a woman. It is, however, important both for the dog and the members of the family that the dog is always the lowest in rank. A dog which works itself up and dominates one or more members of the family will rule the roost. According to the dog's rules it can correct its subordinates by biting without being punished for this and naturally these subordinates do not have as many privileges. This implies that the dog can, for example, forbid the family to enter certain areas in the house and to sit on the sofa. Naturally this leads to an intolerable and dangerous situation in which there are no winners but only losers.

A higher position literally shows that this young Great Dane bitch has a considerably dominant character

Various types of dog

You are now probably wondering why more things do not go wrong if it is in the dog's character to take over if leadership is lacking. One of the reasons for this is that not every dog is born with the mentality to become the leader of the pack. Nature ensures equilibrium by creating dogs that are dominant by nature as well as those with more moderate characters and dogs which by nature are submissive. The differences in disposition can already be seen in the nest and more can be read about this in the chapter "Choosing the right puppy." Many dogs see their masters as the leader of the pack, just because humans tower above dogs and therefore by nature assume a dominant attitude with respect to the dog. If serious mistakes are made in bringing up the dog, not every dog will react to this by taking over the helm. The average family dog becomes unsure in these social circumstances, servile, or aloof. It will only bite in a situation which it experiences as extremely threatening and only when it sees no other way out of the situation. It goes without saying that a dog like this is basically very unhappy.

The leader of the pack

You have a puppy and have thus been thrust into the position of pack leader. From the moment of the dog's arrival you have

As long as the family are still eating, his bowl remains empty

the honor of being the shining example for your dog. A significant part of your dog's reaction to the world around it and its behavior is now in your hands. The pack leader teaches it what it can consider as threatening, really dangerous, or even good fun. The dog will also learn what is permitted and what is not, and will want to repeat the behavior that you approve of, while avoiding behavior of which you disapprove. Your leadership of the pack does not stop after bringing up the pup. It is a continuous process. You, as the leader of the pack, must behave in a manner which commands acceptance and respect. This does not imply that you must present yourself as a stern army officer, but that you must always be clear, fair, and above all consistent toward your dog. This will sometimes mean that you must correct your dog in order to steer its behavior, but how often you will need to do this, and to what extent, is greatly dependent on the disposition of your dog.

Dogs need a fair and consistent pack leader

Right: A Bernese Mountain Dog

Points for attention

There are a few simple, basic, principles, derived from "wolf language," which tell the dog, whatever its innate character traits and without your having to force a critical confrontation, that in your family it holds the lowest rank.

- do not give your dog free access to the whole house. This is the privilege of the rest of the family, because they are higher in rank than the dog. Upstairs is very suitable as "out of bounds" for your dog, also because climbing stairs is not good for its physical condition.
- Do not give the dog its food until everyone else has eaten. The senior in rank always eats first.
- Do not stroke or play with the dog if it tries to make you do so. It is commanding you to pay attention to it and by this awards itself a higher rank.
- Always call the dog to come to you and do not go to it. A superior never goes to a subordinate, but always the reverse.
- When you come home, greet your family first and the dog last. The superior is greeted first, the subordinate last. A condition for a hug or a stroke is that the dog comes to greet you of its own accord.
- Never lie on the floor, always keep your face higher than

Would you like to sit here? A dog that accepts you as the leader would have jumped off the chair long ago

the dog's head. A senior in rank never assumes a lower position than a subordinate during a confrontation.

Signals
So it is very important for your pup to know that it is the lowest in rank in your house. But does it really know that? To find out whether your puppy or (almost) adult dog agrees with the division of roles, you can check the list further on in this chapter. If your dog displays one or more of these traits, then it is taking your leadership with a pinch of salt and you will have to show the dog its rank more clearly. Apply the basic principles for this. If exactly the opposite applies to your dog, then you are dealing with a dog that is well aware of your higher position. It is possible that some forms of behavior only occur with certain members of your family; that will give you an impression of how the dog thinks with respect to that person.

A (much too) dominant dog:
- does not move aside if it is standing or lying in the way. A lower in rank does this only if a higher in rank comes along. So the dog regards itself as higher in rank.
- does not get out of the chair or sofa when you want to sit there. A higher-ranking dog never gives way to a

Rolling on its side or back after a command can be a form of distracting behavior

It's lovely to have a delicious rawhide bone

lower-ranking dog, but vice versa. In addition to this, literally lying on a higher place is confirmation of a higher rank.

- goes through the door into another room before you or jumps in and out of the car before you. The leader is always first, the rest follow.
- pulls at the leash and forces you to follow its direction. In this case too, the dog takes the role of leader and forces you into a subordinate position because you have to follow it.
- pushes its muzzle forcefully against you if it wants to be stroked and becomes more and more persistent if you do not react. This dog is giving you the command "stroke me!" and will react more strongly every time you do not obey its command.
- does not know its own strength, "plays" too roughly, and bites hard. A subordinate will never act too impetuously toward its senior.

Right: This Airedale radiates cheerfulness and sincerity

- will hardly allow normal grooming, such as brushing, and reacts to this by growling. During brushing you are adopting a senior position by standing over it; in the

dog's eyes, you are taking liberties with this intensive physical contact and, on top of this, you are ordering it to stand still.

🦴 Growling is a warning which precedes actual biting; in the dog's eyes, you are overstepping the mark for one who is lower in rank. A subordinate dog accepts grooming from its superior without problems.

Rank

The role of feces and urine in ranking

Dominant males leave their scent markers as high as possible and, in order to achieve this, they contort themselves into the most awkward positions. Young pups of both sexes squat to urinate. Not until roughly the age of puberty do males learn to lift their leg while urinating. From then on, they urinate not only to relieve themselves but also to mark out their territory. Although most bitches continue to urinate in a squatting position, the more dominant ones like to find a higher place to do this. The very dominant ladies even lift one of their back legs while urinating. If a dog feels that he is clearly higher in rank than another, or if he disagrees with the territory boundaries which another male has already set out, he will cover the other dog's scent marker with his own urine. The

The higher the scent mark, the more dominant the maker

place where the feces are deposited says a lot about the dog. High-ranking dogs deposit their feces in a conspicuous spot, preferably on higher ground and the higher the better. Usually it is followed by a lot of scratching about in the ground; the marker's finishing touch to confirm its high rank to other dogs.

Two equal males; their interaction could cause problems, but this can be avoided with good supervision!

Two dogs

Dominance problems between male dogs and bitches do not often occur. The males usually dominate the bitches. Males normally show respect to bitches of the same species. They tolerate much more from them than from males. In a combination of a powerful, dominant bitch and a submissive, weaker male, the bitch sets herself up as the higher in rank. If a dominant bitch and a male that is equally dominant, although smaller and more vulnerable than she is, are kept together, this can create problems. Male dogs which are equally strong and dominant and bitches which are on the same level with regard to size, strength, and disposition often also have problems with rank. Because the ranks are so close to each other, a fight for superiority produces only a temporary winner and his or her high position will, at the first small sign of weakness, be challenged by the lower in rank. This dog will seize the opportunity when the senior in rank becomes sick or infirm or if he or she is punished by the human family in the presence of those lower in rank. Hormonal changes and other situations concerning reproduction, such as the presence of a bitch in heat and a pregnancy, can also give rise to ranking fights. If you want to keep two dogs, observe your present dog's behavior closely and make a conscious choice to prevent problems with ranking. Some breeds are more tolerant than others anyway. Beagles, for example, are known to be tolerant because traditionally they are used to living in packs. Others, including many terriers and some mastiff-type dogs, may show their authority more, which means more chance of squabbles, particularly among male dogs, if you keep more than one dog from this group.

Friends for life
If you already have a dog and the puppy comes into the home as the second dog, after a time a change in the ranking order can occur. As a rule, in the first year the older dog dominates the

They could be lifelong friends, but this depends on their dispositions and your supervision

newcomer. Not until the newcomer reaches puberty is there a changing of the guard, but that is dependent on the characters of both dogs. Many people dislike this. Suddenly the older dog has no more authority and the young madcap is now in charge. It is the first one to eat, steals the chew from the other one, and lays claim to the softest bed. Do not interfere because this does more harm than good. It is better to accept the higher rank of the new dog and to continue to affirm this—even if dog number one also maintains its position. You do this by greeting the higher in rank first, putting its leash on first, giving it its dinner first, and offering it the first chance of a chew or a dog biscuit. Preferably take the higher in rank out for a walk and, if you have to go somewhere with the subordinate, to a show or training, for example, it is better to take the higher in rank along too. The dog which is allowed to go with the owner is higher in rank at that moment than the dog which stays behind to look after the house. When you come home there may be some serious growling, because the lower in rank (supported by you) feels like the king or queen of the castle; and the senior in rank is forced (by you) into a subordinate position. Squabbles of this nature mainly occur in doggy relationships where the ranks are very close together. Good understanding of the ranking among dogs is essential if you have more than one dog.

This Magyar Agar displays a combination of fear and aggression

This young Belgian Shepherd is inviting you to play

Co-operation between two pups; is the owner coming yet?

Children

Dogs and children often make a very good combination. Many dogs instinctively see the child as a "puppy," and from a young child they accept much more than they would normally tolerate. Some dogs, however, do not have this instinct and not all children behave impeccably with respect to dogs. You cannot blame them for this. In their urge to explore, young children can hurt a dog. They do not understand the dog's body language either, such as giving warnings prior to a defensive bite. If something goes wrong, it is neither the fault of the dog nor the child, but of the parents. They should teach a child to have respect for the dog and, if the child is too young to understand, then the parents should ensure that no confrontations arise. Children who are old enough to understand certain things and apply them in practice can be taught the following rules. Teach them that they:

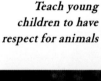 always call the dog to them and never go to the dog themselves;

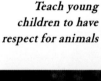 must not scream too loudly, quarrel, or run away, when the dog is around;

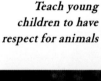 must have respect for the dog, and therefore not:

Teach young children to have respect for animals

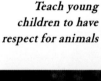 shake the dog to wake it up or take it out of its basket;

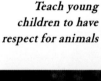 tease it;

 touch its bowl/chewing toy;

- must not give (unnecessary and inconsistent) commands;
- must not lie on the ground, and must always keep their faces higher than the dog's head;
- must never stare at the dog.

Young children cannot be taught all this in one go and therefore, as a precaution, you should never leave young children alone with the dog. It is not possible to say at what age a child is old enough to be left alone with the dog or to take it out. This is dependent on the strength and the character of the dog, and the strength, authority, and sense of responsibility of the child.

Making acquaintance in the street

2 CHOOSING THE RIGHT PUPPY

Inbred characteristics

Dogs are born with a certain disposition and character. Most hounds like to retrieve and love to swim. The average terrier is known to be a noisy show-off and mastiff-type dogs are generally very quiet. If you choose a pedigree dog, you know what the pup will look like when it is an adult, how big it will be, and what characteristics you can expect. These things are established within a breed. And because every breed has characteristics linked to it, you will have to study this subject matter well beforehand. With a good upbringing you can refine a dog's inborn character to a certain extent, but you can never change it. This is not fair toward the dog either, because it is what it is.

Dachshunds have a self-willed but charming character

Right: This young Flat-coated Retriever has the right disposition to become an excellent retriever

You cannot expect from the average terrier that it will sit on your lap all day, just as you cannot expect a Husky to guard your house and home with spirit. It is not in their nature.

Every breed thus has its own inherent characteristics. It would be ideal if, in the first instance, you based your choice of breed on the character traits of that breed and only after that on appearance. A beautiful appearance becomes commonplace after a while, but you never get used to characteristics which do not meet your expectations. Make a list of the characteristics you like in a dog. Does the new housemate have to be a watchdog? Do you want a dog to take for long walks every day or do you prefer one that does not need this? There are countless points on which to select your dog.

Bouvier puppy

Right: The willingness to obey is not very great in a Husky

Breed characteristics

The table below indicates how much exercise is needed by a number of popular breeds of dog and how great their will is to please. If a dog has a low "will to please" score, it implies that this breed can be considerably self-willed. The measure of possible dominance problems that you can expect within your family with this breed is also shown. If a dog has a high score in dominance, this means that you will have to give extra attention to the establishment of rank. A low score in this indicates that most representatives of this breed pose little or no problems with ranking. The scores relate to the average characteristics for that breed. Much will depend on how closely the parents and ancestors of your new housemate represent the average breed profile in the area of character; response, socialization, and upbringing are also of great importance. The table is far from complete. Since there are more than four hundred breeds of dog, it is impossible to treat all breeds in this way. You can find information about these in the various books which are devoted specifically to the subject.

The mongrel's character is not so easy to predict

	Amount of exercise	Dominance	Will to please
(German, Belgian) Shepherd	+++	+++/++++	++++
Collie (Rough)	+++	++	+++/++++
Bobtail	+++	+/++	+++
Rottweiler	+++	++++	++/+++
Bouvier	+++	+++	+++
Doberman	+++/++++	++++	++/+++
Terriers	+++	++++	++
Husky	++++	++	+
Beagle	+++	++	+
Dachshund	+++	+++	+
Spaniel	+++	++	+++
Retrievers	++++	++	++++
Newfoundland	++	++	++
Great Dane	+++	++/+++	++
St. Bernard	++	++/+++	++
English Bulldog	+	+	++
Boxer	++++	+++	+++
Maltese	++	+	+++
German Pointer	++++	+++	+++

+	= less than average
++	= average
+++	= more than average
++++	= a lot

Mongrels

The character of mongrels and cross-breeds is inherently present at birth. The disadvantage of these dogs is that the character cannot be predicted very well. If you know both the father and the mother, then you have an indication, but sometimes only the mother is known or neither of the parents. Cross-breeds are dogs of which both the mother and the father are pedigree dogs but each of a different breed. If it concerns a cross between the same sort of dog, for example a cross between a Whippet and a Greyhound, then the pups have an unmistakable Greyhound character. If you like Greyhounds then this would be a good choice for you. It is different if it concerns a cross between a Husky and a Labrador Retriever, or a Boxer and an Afghan Hound. These breeds differ from each other on many points, not only in appearance, but also in character. The eventual character of the pup from this sort of cross is very difficult to forecast. Although cross-breeds are mostly unusual in appearance, the purchase of an animal of this kind is inadvisable for anyone with clear-cut ideas regarding the character of their new housemate.

Dominant pups

You can see the differences in character while pups are still in the nest. The first pup which comes toward you has the greatest self-confidence and the most spunk. This puppy does not allow you to turn it on its back, or only with difficulty, and carries its tail high. It is usually a show-off and has the whole litter in tow. It is the future leader of the pack and is best suited to an owner who can stand his/her ground. These dogs make the best watchdogs because they are not easily impressed by anything. Do not buy a dog like this unless you have wide experience with dogs. This kind of dog does not belong in a family with young children or with people who are inconsistent and/or too lenient.

Most Rottweilers have an inherent dominant character

Right: "Shy" puppies need much more encouragement and praise than others

The shy puppy

The pups that tend to stay in the background and, when you approach them, fold their ears back and make themselves small are dogs which need a lot of encouragement and appreciation because they do not have much confidence by nature. They lick your hand, quickly turn over, and lie on their back and are rather cringing. If you turn a pup like this on its back, it often remains there even after you have taken your hand away. This is the type of dog that functions best in quiet surroundings and can be brought up gently and with a lot of loving care. A stern or inconsistent upbringing in a very busy environment turns this kind of mild-mannered puppy into a neurotic dog. For these dogs the emphasis should be on rewarding good behavior. They blossom on "good boy" and "well done". Normally you can punish the dog with your voice. A slip collar will probably not even be necessary. It is very important for these dogs that they are extremely well-socialized.

This Old English Bulldog pup looks at the world through shrewd eyes

The "average" pup

Puppies that joyfully come to you, but do not behave with exaggerated freedom like the more dominant ones of the litter, form the average group. They let you turn them onto their backs, but get up again as soon as you take your hand away. They have an open and happy character and are on average the most suitable family pets. With a normal upbringing they grow into sociable, uncomplicated pals.

Labrador Retriever puppy

Golden-retriever pup

3 RESPONSE AND SOCIALIZATION PHASES

Response

An extremely important phase in the life of a dog is the response phase, which takes place from the third up to about the seventh week. In view of the fact that puppies are normally not taken from their mothers before the age of about eight weeks, your pup will have gone through this phase at the breeder's. Hopefully, he or she knew what they were doing, because the wrong coaching during this crucial phase leads to permanent disturbances in behavior. Basically, during the response phase the pup begins to experience the world around

Your pup sees you as its shining example and attunes its reactions to yours

Top right: If pups are frequently held in the hands at a young age, they become used to contact with people more quickly

Below right: Two English Bulldog pups of a few weeks old

it. It hears the sound of the television, the vacuum cleaner, and children playing, and learns that these sounds are not threatening. It is picked up, cuddled, and stroked by (strange) people and children and, as long as this acquaintance is made in a friendly way, it learns that people are a part of its life and do it no harm. Puppies born and brought up indoors in the living room or kitchen do not need extra response training. They are in daily contact with the world—this is normal for them.

If they are kept in a kennel or an isolated area, it is the breeder's task to bring the pups into regular contact with normal, everyday life. It is not necessary to expose them for hours to stimuli and impressions; twenty minutes a day is enough for good response. Pups that have undergone proper response training in this very important phase of their lives have a sound basis from which to develop into stable, adult dogs.

Kennel syndrome

The impressions gained by the animals during this phase stay with them for the rest of their lives. In other words, what is done during this period can never be undone. If a pup is brought up in isolation in a kennel or shed where it has

Socialize your dog with cattle too

received little or no stimuli, it will later display chronically disordered, antisocial behavior. The dog suffers from what is known as "kennel syndrome." These dogs are extremely nervous and wary of our well-meant care. When approached, they try to make themselves scarce, and if this does not succeed will drop their tail between their legs. Their eyes are glassy, their ears laid back, and they often pass some drops of urine or roll over onto their back. They are terrified by the noise of the television or passing traffic and will try to run away. This behavior occurs again and again, even though the television is on the whole day or cars are going by continuously.

It goes without saying that these dogs are desperately unhappy. They live in a world which is, quite simply, terrifying to them. Any attempts to approach them on your part, however friendly, are experienced as frightening and the same holds for all other impressions which they missed out on or barely received during the response phase.

> In order to prevent a dog from developing kennel syndrome, it needs to experience very many different things during the critical response phase (3rd to 7th week).

Experiencing new things takes a lot of energy

Socialization

The socialization phase follows the response phase and continues until the age of approximately 14 weeks. The former is similar to the latter, but with one significant difference: a dog that has had inadequate socialization can function reasonably well later. An enormous amount of patience and insight is required for this, however, with inadequate socialization always having to be paid for in the end because, in spite of all the efforts put in later, the dog will never display 100 percent well-adjusted behavior. Apart from this, there is one other important difference: this phase hardly ever occurs at the breeder's, but in your home. It is up to you to ensure that your dog is well socialized. See to it that your dog gets acquainted in a positive way with a variety of widely differing situations, animals, strangers, children, and city traffic, and all kinds of sounds. The more positive impressions the dog has experienced, the more well-balanced its reactions will be to later situations and the better it will eventually function as a family pet. Next to the response phase, the socialization phase is the most important of the dog's life.

You should avoid this kind of confrontation during the response and socialization phases

A sensitive stage of life

Your pup will react in a stable manner to all that it experienced as non-threatening in the socialization stage. The reverse also applies. If your pup has very negative experiences somewhere along the line during this phase, for the rest of its life it will react with fear, or aggression, and certainly unpredictably in a similar situation. If, for example, it is bitten by another dog, this experience will have a negative effect on its development in relation to other dogs. How strongly this affects the dog in later life, however, mainly depends on your reaction to it. You are your dog's shining example, so a large part of its reaction depends on your behavior. The worst thing that you can do is to comfort it or become panicky. This just confirms to the pup that it has reason to be afraid. What the dog has experienced becomes fixed in its memory and, when confronted with a subsequent comparable situation, it will react with panic. Thus you are dealing with a maladjusted, frightened dog. Depending on its disposition, during future confrontations it will either hide away or go on the attack. It goes without saying that, with such a dog, pleasant walks are not an option.

What can you do to prevent this problem developing? If your dog is scared by something or you notice hesitation on its part in encountering a situation that is new to it, react resolutely and with self assurance to the experience. You are the boss, the leader, and the example for the pup, and you decide what is scary and what is not. Totally ignore its frightened behavior, walk on, and give a tug on the leash to urge your dog to walk on also and stop behaving foolishly. You will notice that your dog adopts your self-confident attitude and that this ameliorates the effect of what it has just experienced.

This Chihuahua thinks the cat is definitely scary

Normally, rabbits are prey, but nowadays they are often housemates for our dog

Foresight is the essence of government

During the socialization phase, it is good to acquaint your dog with as many situations and animals as possible. A dog can live to the age of 10 or more and you cannot see into the future. For example, though you might not have a cat and perhaps even hate cats, you should still socialize your dog with a friendly cat. Maybe you will have a cat at some time or get a new partner who loves cats. Bridges, public transport, and elevators are a similar issue. If you live in the town, your dog will automatically get used to children playing, traffic, and bustle but, if this is not the case, take the dog to the town with you during its socialization phase so that it can experience these things. In country surroundings, your dog will become familiar with cattle and other farm animals as a matter of course, but in other cases you can take the dog to a children's farm to make acquaintance with the animals there. By using the socialization phase to the full you can prevent long-term problems. Do not overdo it though, because too many experiences all at once are too much for a young pup.

4 THE BASIC PRINCIPLES FOR TRAINING AND UPBRINGING

Right: Your dog must understand why it is being rewarded

Rewarding

In your dog's upbringing, make use of the principles of reward and punishment. We give a reward when the dog does something that we would like to see repeated. The essence of reward is that it gives the dog a good feeling. Because it gets that good feeling from a certain action or exercise, it will enjoy repeating it. In rewarding, two things are important:

➤ The dog must understand that it is being rewarded;
➤ The dog must understand why it is being rewarded.

This would seem to be a natural conclusion, but in practice it does not seem to be so obvious. How often is a dog rewarded with only a mumbled "Good boy" and a nonchalant pat on the head? Or a morsel is thrown at it without a word being wasted? You can tell from the dog's reaction whether this is experienced as a reward. Its entire body and expression should radiate joy. You can achieve this by rewarding your dog lavish-

At around this endearing age, it is sometimes difficult to say "No!"

ly with a high voice and a sincere hug. When it does something good, it is the best dog in the world and you must let it know this too! Many people find this difficult, especially when other people are around. Don't be shy about this, because with a clear reward your dog will learn faster.

The moment of rewarding must be well-timed. You do not reward before your dog has obeyed a command and neither do you do it afterward. If, for example, you want your dog to lie down, do not reward it at the moment it starts to obey, but only when it is actually lying down.

Punishing

For punishing, the same applies as rewarding, in effect. By punishing the dog in the correct way for misbehavior, it will refrain from doing this sooner. Doing something that is not permitted only produces feelings of unease in the dog and the desire to do something wrong becomes less strong. Also, when punishing your dog you must ensure that the pup fully understands that it is being punished and why. You can continually shout "Naughty!" but, if you make a habit of this, your pup will learn that you often say something which it does not need to take notice of. The words "Naughty" or "No" lose their meaning. Young dogs can usually be brought to order with your voice. Most of them are swiftly impressed by "Naughty," spoken angrily in a deep voice. In addition to this, larger or more stubborn dogs can be corrected with a slip collar by giving a short and very clear tug on the leash. If your dog just walks on or hardly reacts, it is possible that it either did not hear or understand your command or that it does not accept your authority.

"Caught in the act" punishment

You should always give punishment at the moment itself, and never afterward. Your dog associates your punishment specifically with what it is doing at that moment. If, for example, it has just torn up your newspaper but is now running up to you joyfully wagging its tail, it has now completely forgotten about the newspaper.

At that moment, the overpowering fact is that your dog wants to make contact with you and is glad to see you and you react to that with punishment... Your dog does not understand this and will adopt a subordinate (frightened) manner to show you that you are higher in rank, in order to stop your aggression toward it. This behavior is all too often wrongly interpreted by the owner as guilty behavior. If you punish the dog now, you are making a big mistake in upbringing. Older dogs, particularly the more dominant ones, become defensive, certainly at a moment like this. They growl or bite because they are being treated unjustly and, even though they are in the right, it is the

To prevent your dog from getting up to mischief and your continually having to punish it, ensure that there is as little opportunity as possible of temptation. Opportunity makes the thief. An indoor kennel can be a valuable help here. Saying "No" and "Naughty" too often does not improve the mutual understanding between you and your dog.

thin end of the wedge for them. It is also unwise to remain angry with your dog. Going on grumbling is something that the dog cannot understand. If it does something wrong, punish it "in the act." If the dog obeys after this, it is always a "Good boy" (or "girl").

Correcting with the aid of a slip collar

The slip collar is an ideal means of correcting your dog. Wolves correct each other with a short, sharp bite in the neck. If a slip collar is used in the correct way, it has the same effect on a dog and is understood well. You put it on the dog as shown in the photo. A chain put on this way slackens as soon as you stop pulling on it. If the chain is put on the other way round, it often stays tight. This makes the dog uncomfortable and you cannot

correct it properly in this manner. Neither can you correct it properly when the leash is kept taut. All you do then is to pull the dog along a little bit, but the effect of a "bite" is lost. You only achieve this when the slip collar stays loosely around the dog's neck and you then give it a short, sharp, but clearly felt tug.

Various types of slip collars

There are various types of slip collar. They vary from very thin links to large oval links. The fine, thin links are the most suitable for pups from the age of about three to seven months.

From seven months onward you can give your dog a chain made of large, oval links. The advantage of the large oval links is that can you "lock" these into a piston clip, so that the chain has a double function. You can also use it as an ordinary, non-choker collar. The larger links are less damaging to the neck hair. Quite often, hair gets caught in the small links. That irritates the dog and this can result in a partially bare neck. A slip collar, by the way, is only worn during training or walking in the period of upbringing. Indoors it is better not to put a chain on your dog at all. During long walks in the wood too, when your dog can frolic about freely, a chain of this kind can be dangerous because it can easily get caught on something.

It is better not to use a metal slip collar until your dog is three months old; a nylon slip collar is more suitable. The chance that you will need to correct your pup before then with a slip collar or slip chain is very small.

Shaking prey

Many a dog owner thinks that a dog can best be shaken by the scruff of the neck. There are even books on bringing up dogs which propagate this! Never, however, make the mistake of "punishing" your dog in this way. Wolves and dogs only display this behavior to kill their prey, but never to correct one of

Halter

Spiked collar

their own species. Your dog will understand from this that you see it as prey and will not know how to handle this situation. The effect of hitting and other non-canine punishments will also be greatly to reduce its confidence in you.

Alternative aids

A number of alternative aids have been developed. They cannot replace the slip chain and are not intended for this. One of the most effective aids is the dog halter. This ensures that, during daily walks, you can keep your dog well under control with a minimum of strength. The dog halter is not suitable for bringing up or training the dog, but is extremely useful for strong adult dogs with a chronic pulling problem or those which, time and again, lunge out at other dogs. For dogs like this these a spiked collar was used in the past, but that only made the problem worse because most dogs become insensitive in their neck after a time. What applies to the slip chain also applies to the halter. It must be used with care.

Consistency

The success of your bringing up and how you get on with your dog depends on the measure to which you are consistent. You can socialize your dog perfectly, but without consistency the effect of your efforts will be minimal. If you are inconsistent, your dog will be confused. It is totally unclear to the dog why it may snuggle up closely to you on the sofa today and tomorrow it is not allowed, and the fact that yesterday you did not mind it barking while today you punish it for the same behavior. Maintaining flexible rules in the house is confusing for a dog and for a dominant dog such a changeable method constitutes a reason to try to snatch power. Other dogs become unsure or ignore your commands more often.

It is extremely difficult to be consistent. Nearly always, being consistent means that in the end you are not consistent. Being consistent is continuous and implies that anything you permit the dog to do, you must always permit, and anything you forbid, you must always forbid. To keep this up requires not only effort from you, but also from the rest of the family and everyone must keep to it. It means that, even before the pup arrives, you and your family must agree together about what you do and do not allow. Is the dog allowed to lie on the sofa, sleep on the bed, jump up at people? You must discuss these things beforehand.

This boxer is rather confused. Its name is being called from two sides. Who should it listen to?

Commands

You must be consistent in everything, including training. Do not, for example, relinquish a command given earlier. This sort of situation occurs when you order your dog to "Sit" at the edge of the pavement, but almost immediately you see that no traffic is coming and you urge it to walk on. Do not accept a half-obeyed command. If, for example, you give the dog the command "Down" and, after long lingering and being aggravating, it finally sits down, it is not yet "Good dog", even if you are tired of training at that moment. It is not "Good dog" until it has carried out your command. Cancelling an earlier command also comes into this category. Cancelling a command can only be done by the one who has given the command. You can teach the dog a word for this, such as "OK then" or "Easy."

Do not tell your dog to go to its basket if you cannot check whether it does so

Let your dog have a romp between exercises; all work and no play makes Jack a dull boy

Do not demand too much

You ordered your dog into its basket and it obeyed quickly. After five minutes, it jumps happily out of its basket. It has now cancelled your command. In a normal domestic situation it is, however, extremely difficult, if not impossible, to see that it continues to lie in its basket. There are so many other things that require your attention. Therefore, only give a command which you can check on. Do not tell the dog to go into its basket when you leave the room, but put it in its indoor kennel. Your dog does not then need to be disobedient and you do not need to be inconsistent. For the same reason, only give your dog a command which it has thoroughly learned. At the stage in which your pup still has everything to learn, you are teaching it through play, but when it is so well advanced that it knows a certain command well, then it has absolutely no excuse for not doing it. Prevent disobedience by not expecting too much from the dog. No dog succeeds in concentrating on the exercises for a whole hour. Mistakes will creep in, because you demanded more than it could give.

Recognizing distracting behavior

A well-known term in modern canine psychology is "distracting behavior." The dog has an inner conflict; it is heartily sick of the training but does not want to incur your displeasure. Instead of following up your command at once, it goes away to urinate, yawns, or lies on its back and rolls over. If your dog displays this behavior, play with it for a few minutes and close off the exercise with a command it knows well and obeys well. Stop training after this. If your dog displays a lot of distracting behavior, make the training sessions shorter and more varied.

Preventing problem behavior

Distracting behavior chiefly manifests itself in big yawns

It is very important that, while your pup is still so open and impressionable, you immediately put a stop to any negative characteristics or behavior. Continuous, unnecessary barking, jumping up at people, whining during a car journey, chasing

cats, and aggressive reactions to the mailman are things which, if not radically tackled, grow to be habits which are difficult for the dog to break. If you invest a lot of time the first year in preventing this problem behavior, your efforts will be more than rewarded.

Never tolerate your dog chasing after other animals or barking at them

The boss has my full attention

5 YOUR PUPPY IN THE HOME

A place of its own

Your puppy needs its own place to go to in the house—somewhere it can always lie undisturbed. A young puppy in particular will make good use of this, because it still needs a lot of sleep. This place can be a basket, a mattress, a cushion, or a dog bed. Whatever you use as a bed, remember that puppies are at the "discovering" stage and they will certainly investigate whether their bed can be torn up and how it tastes. If, at a young age, a dog has experienced what fun it is to pick a mattress or a soft cushion to pieces, it will continue to do this later. Therefore, a basket or a soft cushion are not suitable for a puppy. A hard plastic bed or a strong dog bench is a better choice, but the best is an indoor kennel. The choice of bed for

A cushion to lie on

A wicker basket is not suitable for young pups

This Smooth-haired Collie is satisfied with its comfortable dog bed

Right: Bobtail

Large, short-haired breeds soon get ugly patches of hard skin from lying on a surface which is too hard

the puppy is particularly important for large, short-coated breeds. They need a soft bed to prevent ugly hard skin from forming on the joints and other pressure points. It is impossible for you to provide a comfortable bed if your dog continually picks it to pieces. It is better to wait until it has passed through adolescence before you introduce beds of this kind. You could buy two beds, which will give you the opportunity to let the dog into the living room during the day and evening and at night into the kitchen or laundry room, for example. Particularly while your dog is not completely house trained or chews things up in its urge to explore, having a bed in the kitchen or some place else where it can do no damage is ideal. Use a blanket that is machine-washable for the basket. A loose

If you buy an indoor kennel or bench to allow for growing, you will get more use from it

blanket has the advantage that you can take it with you when you take your dog along on a visit. You then always have a temporary but familiar "bed" with you for your dog.

Indoor kennel(s)

The usefulness of an indoor kennel has been known for years. In the past, it was mostly breeders who bought indoor kennels, but fortunately nowadays more and more private owners have realized that an indoor kennel is very useful, if not indispensable, for house training and the prevention of problem behavior. A good, sturdy indoor kennel is not cheap, especially in the larger sizes, but it will pay for itself in the long run because, when in its indoor kennel, your dog will not get the chance to sink its teeth into your furniture or soil your carpet. An extra advantage is that you never need to be angry with your dog when you come home, which is good for mutual bonding.

There are people who think it is a shame to put a dog in a kennel. It certainly is a shame if the dog has to stay in its indoor kennel for too long just because of your laziness. This, however, is up to you. To ensure that your dog thinks of its indoor kennel as a safe "den", make the kennel as interesting as possible by putting toys, chews, and a soft blanket in it. Do not put the dog in it for punishment or leave it in the kennel unnecessarily long. It is an aid to upbringing and not a dog cage. Most dogs show that they like their indoor kennel, by often going there when they feel the need for rest.

Pekingese

A place of its own

The basket or indoor kennel is a place to which the dog can withdraw without being disturbed. Therefore, do not keep moving the basket from one place to another. Tell your children that the basket is not a toy for them and that they must not disturb the dog whenever it is in its basket. It is the dog's only form of privacy, which must be respected. The best place for a basket is an area where the family spend most of their time. A second basket or indoor kennel can be put in another room such as a kitchen, laundry room, or in the hall.

If you want to take away a chew, exchange it for a tasty morsel

The first night

The first night in your house can be a frightening experience for your dog. Up till now, its world has consisted of its mother, brothers, and sisters, and now it is suddenly alone. It also misses all the comfortable, familiar smells. It is ideal if the breeder has given you a piece of blanket from the nest. You can put that in its kennel to ease its distress a little. Not all dogs, but some of them, whine the first night and sometimes the second night too. This whining has nothing to do with human crying. It is a rallying signal, through which your dog is trying to make contact. It is feeling lonely and wants to end the loneliness by whining. If you pay attention to its calling, you are rewarding it for undesirable behavior. There is a big chance that your dog will continue to start whining again if it does not want to be alone, even when you just pop out to do some shopping. In any case, it makes no difference whether you go to the dog to comfort it, scold it, or just call out from your bed to rebuke or console it. It was seeking contact and found it. Ignoring whining is—understandably—very difficult for some people, but if you persevere you will prevent future problems.

Some people let their dog sleep in a box next to their bed for the first week and stroke it or comfort it if it whines. The advantage of this is that you are in time if your dog wants to relieve itself, but there are disadvantages to this as well. Sooner

Howling is a rallying call

or later it will have to get used to sleeping alone, and moreover you are allowing it to be in a room which, later on, it will no longer be allowed to enter.

Keeping watch

Keeping watch means that your dog makes itself heard if something unusual happens around the house. This should not be confused with defending, whereby the dog actually physically confronts an intruder. Most dogs naturally keep watch and need no encouragement to do this. If you have a dog which is too socially-oriented and you would be only too pleased if it barked when something happened, you can achieve this by drawing the dog's attention every time there is someone at the front door. If you have a pup from a breed which is well known for its watchful character, it is better not to do this, because you will be cultivating a dog with an exaggerated barking habit, which will make you no friends in the vicinity of your home. Be patient with a social dog like this. The watchful instinct develops naturally as the dog gets older and you therefore do not need to be worried if your dog of four or five months old hardly makes itself heard. There are dogs that will barely react when everyone is at home but will definitely start to bark when they are keeping watch alone, because there is nobody else to keep watch then.

Behavior and habits

Barking
Some breeds are more inclined to bark than others. Nobody minds when a dog barks if there is something wrong. Burglars in particular may be announced loudly and clearly; that is what a dog is for. We get a feeling of security that our dog is keeping watch during the night. It is another matter if it continues to bark even when the mailman is in the next street or your visitors have already been in the house for some time. Some dogs also bark when they see a cat or another dog passing by. If you live in a residential area, it should be your highest priority to

Golden Retriever puppy

ensure that your dog does not bark any more than necessary. If
the dog responds to your voice, give it the command "Quiet!"
if it barks unnecessarily. Say it in a low and angry tone. Say the
dog's name first, so that it knows who you are speaking to. If
the dog is so beside itself that your voice does not make much
impression, the best way to correct this behavior is with the slip
chain. You should then not say anything to the dog, so do not
praise it when it becomes quiet. Your dog will remember that
barking results in an uncomfortable feeling (the jerk on the
slip chain) and it will not do this so quickly in the future. Dogs
that see every passer-by as a reason to jump up, barking, onto
the window-sill or sofa can also be corrected in this manner.

The mailman

The fact that most dogs, however quiet they are normally and
however friendly they are toward visitors, can explode into
such aggression toward the man or woman who delivers your
mail, does have a logical explanation. The mailman comes to
your house every day. The dog reacts to this by barking; after
all, the mailman is in the dog's territory and does not belong to
the pack. The barking is successful: the mailman walks away.
In the eyes of your dog, the mailman has fled because of the

barking. This strengthens the dog's self-confidence, causing it to bark even more frantically. The problem is that this reaches a point at which habit-forming occurs. The solution is as logical as it is simple: forbid your dog to bark at the mailman right from the beginning, in the same manner as you would normally do if it continues to bark.

Jumping up to people

It is such a nice sight: a sweet puppy with dark eyes like beads and a shiny black nose, who joyfully jumps up at your visitors. Remember, however, that, if you do not soon stop it from doing this, it will continue to do so, when it is an adolescent dog (and therefore not so sweet), has muddy feet, or when you are just about to go to a party. A dog cannot tell the difference between your special clothes and jeans; neither can it read your thoughts. Yesterday you liked this and even played with it for a short while, but today you are annoyed with your dog for jumping up and punish it for this. What is the dog to make of this? Therefore, be consistent from day one. You either allow it or you do not allow it. You can teach your dog not to do this by ensuring that it associates this with something negative. Usually giving it a sharp push with your knee works well. Do not push it away with your hand and do not say anything friendly or unfriendly. This would be paying more attention

Golden Retriever puppy

than is desired. It is best to ignore this undesired behavior completely. Try to prevent your dog from going wrong when you arrive home, by squatting down to stroke and hug the dog. You then remove the necessity for it to jump up. If, on the one hand, there is no necessity to jump up at you and, on the other, jumping up brings negative reactions, the dog will stop doing it.

Smart cookies

There are some very smart dogs that can really try your patience. In no time, they manage to open the kitchen cupboards or doors to other parts of the house. There are even some dogs who have no problem with opening the ice box door, who can turn lever faucets on (but not off!), and can turn lights on and off. The best thing you can do about this is to ensure that your dog develops a negative association with these things, without linking this with your presence. You could, for example, make a loud noise at the moment the dog is doing something wrong. It is, however, not easy to catch your dog

Chow-Chow puppy

red-handed every time, give it a fright, and keep out of the picture yourself. Furthermore, this requires a specific approach which can be different for every dog.

The easiest way is to ensure that your dog simply does not get the chance to do anything wrong. If you cannot keep an eye on things, put the dog in a kennel either indoors or outside. Make it impossible for the dog to open doors by fitting round knobs which have to be turned or putting a lock on the door. But remember: your dog obviously has an above-average IQ and enjoys solving problems. Perhaps it is bored and the daily walks provide so little mental stimulation that it looks for challenges indoors. Go to an agility course or obedience training with the dog, or make up little games to play with it, like hide and seek, tracking, retrieving, and short, varied obedience exercises.

Begging
Begging for biscuits or for your dinner is a very irritating habit which you teach the dog yourself. If you never give it anything to eat outside training and its food bowl, it will know that begging produces no results and will cease to do it. Remember that your dog will become more persistent in this behavior if you give it something now and then to be free of its whining and appealing gaze. It will specifically learn from this inconsistency that, if it perseveres stubbornly, a reward will eventually follow. And your dog has all the time in the world.

Problems around the feeding bowl
The feeding bowl occupies a special place in the hearts of many dogs. Some of them are so crazy about food that they growl at people who come too close, because they might perhaps have come to take the food away. If its greatest fear is realized, a dog can let fly. To prevent your dog from growling near the feeding bowl, begin by teaching the young puppy that it is alright if you or some other member of the family takes the bowl away for a short while. Put a few extra biscuits in it or a piece of sausage or cheese and give it back at once. In this way the puppy learns that, when you take its bowl away, something tasty comes back in it and this removes the reason to growl.

Care and grooming

Teeth
Dogs exchange their milk teeth for their permanent teeth between the ages of about four to seven months. Because at

around this age dogs have a greater need to chew than normal, it is important that you provide plenty of opportunity for chewing during this period. For older dogs, too, it is important that they have something to chew at least once a week and preferably more frequently. In this way you prevent teeth problems developing when your dog is older.

Always give your dog a safe bone to chew; one that is too large is better than one that is too small, and it should be tough. Pressed buffalo hide is a very suitable option.

Care of the coat

How often you should brush and comb your dog depends on the structure and length of its coat. Dogs with a coat needing

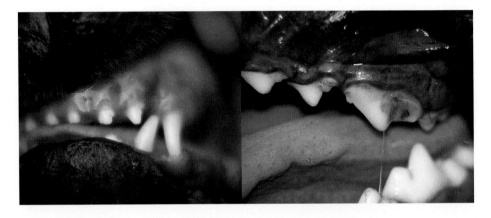

Milk teeth

Right: An adult dog's teeth affected by tartar

a lot of care, such as the Bobtail and Afghan Hound, need more attention than short-haired breeds. If you have a dog with a long coat, grooming will form an essential part of its daily care. It is of the greatest importance for these breeds that you get your puppy used to this as soon as possible, because neglect of the coat can lead to skin irritations, abscesses, and worse. Wherever you have your dog groomed, they can tell you tales about dogs which are brought in with matted fur, resulting in suffocated skin with wounds and abscesses. The condition of these dogs is not necessarily due to deliberate neglect by the owners, but is more often due to the dog's strong resistance to being groomed. After one struggle, the owner gives up out of sympathy for the dog. It goes without saying that you should prevent these extreme situations. You do this by acquainting your dog with brushing, combing, and trimming from a very early age. Teach it to stand on a table with a rough surface, so that it cannot slip. A rubber mat usually works very well. Brush and comb your dog's coat layer by layer, but make sure

Catch them while they are young

Cutting the nails

you do not hurt it and thereby cause it to develop a hatred of the process. If you do this in the right way, your dog will have no reason to whine or struggle, and you should not allow this behavior. Do not, by the way, make the mistake of comforting the puppy if, by accident, you do hurt it. This would confirm that something bad has happened and, as a consequence, your dog will resist the following brushing session more strongly.

Demolishing
Ruining your possessions can be due to various reasons. The most usual causes are boredom and the need to chew. Boredom occurs when a dog has too little exercise, or attention,

Inspecting the ear canal

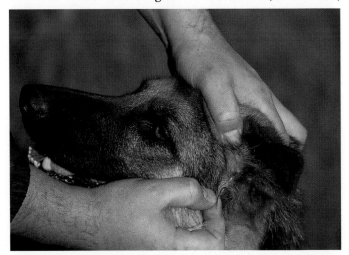

or too few things to do. Breeds which are "made" to run about or be active in one way or another have more problems than other dogs if they have to be in the house all day. By compensating for these shortcomings with activities and exercise for the dog— thereby giving your dog the requisite attention— there will no longer be any reason for this behavior.

All dogs have a need to chew. Chewing on a safe, rawhide bone not only helps to keep their teeth healthy but also provides distraction. See to it that your dog always has something to chew, so that it does not hit on the idea of trying out the legs of the chair or your three-piece suite. At the age when they are losing their puppy teeth and getting their permanent ones—between the ages of about four to seven months—pups also have more need to chew. Finally, there are some dogs which have always behaved perfectly and suddenly develop destructive behavior during puberty, which can occur at different ages according to the breed. As long as there are no signs of boredom or any other frustrations, destruction is a temporary problem. It is

Combing and brushing your dog daily or weekly is good for its coat. You will discover possible irregularities, ticks, and small wounds sooner; moreover, the act of brushing confirms your superior rank.

not practical to punish your dog for this, particularly when the damage has been done during your absence. Avoid this developing into a dislike for your dog by not giving it a chance to destroy your things. An indoor kennel is a big help in this situation.

The vet

A visit to the vet is very unpleasant for many dogs. After all, your dog can expect a thorough examination, a vaccination, or something else that it dislikes. In addition to this, your dog has a sharp sense of smell and at the vet's it will pick up a great variety of most unusual scents. Exaggeratedly frightened behavior though is usually not the result of some painful treatment or series of treatments, but of your comforting reaction to this. The same applies at the vet's as during socialization: if you give your dog the idea that this is the most normal thing in the world—and it is—and definitely do not comfort it, the effect of a potentially painful treatment will have less impact on the dog.

For the lack of a suitable bone, dogs look for something to satisfy their urge to chew

Toy and chewing article in one

Various chewing toys

6 HOUSE TRAINING

The first steps

During the first weeks of the puppy's life, the mother cleans up all the feces and urine produced by her offspring. She continues to do this until the puppies have been weaned. If the breeder has provided a "nest" in which the mother and babies can rest and sleep, and an adjoining pen where they can play, most of the feces will be deposited outside the nest. No mentally fit dog would dream of soiling its bed, because that is contrary to its nature.

Exceptions to this are puppies which grow up at a breeder's who has little room, does not clean up enough of the feces and urine, or where there is a combination of both factors. The animals then become so used to soiled surroundings that in the end it is normal to them. It is often very difficult to house-train these dogs. Normally, dogs are "clean" by nature. The only thing you have to teach them is that not only their basket but the rest of the house too must be treated as their nest.

The dam cleans up all the feces and urine from her pups until they have been weaned

Do not expect too much

Even though a puppy appears to be house-trained, it is still possible for it to "make a mistake" now and then. This is very understandable and nothing to get angry about. Young dogs do not yet have full control over their bladders. Mistakes do happen sometimes, especially at night. You must not blame

Right: A Dalmatian puppy

your dog for this. At around the age of five to six months an average dog has enough control, so that this normally no longer occurs. If your puppy does still frequently urinate in the house, make an appointment with the vet. It is possible that there is a problem, such as a bladder infection.

Prevention is better than cure
Dogs have very sensitive noses, which enables them to analyze all kinds of scents which are unrecognizable to us. They can localize the scent of "jobs" which have been done earlier, even right through the most penetrating smell of strong cleaning agents. A dog is a creature of habit and when it needs to do its "job" it often visits the same place again to do this. By preventing your dog from going wrong indoors as much as possible, you are thus preventing a repeat of the offence. It goes without saying that following your puppy around for the first few weeks will take a lot of your time and energy, but your efforts will be amply rewarded by a puppy which is soon house-trained. If you see your dog sniffing at the ground or turning around in small circles, that is a sign that something is on its way. Do not call it to come outside—the urge can become too strong on the way—but pick the dog up and put it down outside. Of course, you will praise it lavishly if it continues its unfinished business there. If you cannot be on guard for a while, the indoor kennel is a blessing.

The right moment
In principle, you can assume that a puppy gets the urge after having slept or eaten. It is definitely not overdone to let your puppy out at least once every hour in the beginning, to give it

Through the recognizable scent, a puppy always gets the urge to relieve itself at the same spot

the chance to relieve itself. Give the dog a chance to relieve itself as late as possible in the evening and in the morning be prompt in letting the dog go outside again. The shorter the night, the better. Remove the water bowl for the night and let the dog start the night with its bowels as empty as possible.

Infections
The best place for your dog to learn to do its job is your own garden. Special dog toilets, which in some places you are obliged to make use of, are taboo until your dog has been fully vac-

cinated. Until they have had their final vaccination, puppies are still susceptible to various—sometimes fatal—diseases. They become infected with these in parks and other places which are regularly visited by other dogs. Sometimes, just sniffing the feces of a strange dog is enough to make your pup ill. If you have no garden yourself, try to find a green area near your house which you know is not used by many dogs.

Rewarding
Just as your dog can get into repetitive behavior indoors, so it can outside. Make use of your dog's excellent sense of smell by taking it again and again to the same place outside where it relieved itself before. Never forget to praise your dog generously when it does "a job" outside. You have to show that you are exceptionally proud of it. Your dog will then be inclined to repeat the action. Praising is much more important than punishment when house training your dog.

Punishment

It is quite understandable that you want to punish your dog when it makes a mistake indoors, but it is much better not to do this. If you punish your dog after catching it red-handed, it could get the idea that it must not defecate in your sight. The result of this is that your dog finds ways to defecate and urinate at moments when you are not looking and in places where you are unlikely to see it. These dogs will happily walk alongside you on the leash for an hour and when you get home they will find a quiet place behind the sofa or under the table. So punishment often has an adverse effect, both when catching the dog red-handed or afterward. Once the deed has been done, punishment is of no use at all. You know that your dog associates the punishment with what it is doing at that moment. It is also totally useless to rub its nose in it to make clear why you are angry. Rewarding good behavior and preventing accidents works better and faster and avoids countless problems in this area. If you see your dog doing something wrong, pick the dog up and put it outside without saying anything. If it continues to "perform" outside, praise the dog lavishly.

"Doing jobs" on command

It may sound a bit strange, teaching your dog to urinate or defecate on command. After all, a dog is not a machine. And yet, this is easier for a dog to learn than you might think. In

A dog can easily be taught to defecate "on command"

Bitches urinate in a squatting position; males do this until they reach puberty

these times, when fouling the sidewalks is a source of great annoyance for many and is leading to a stricter and more unbending local government policy regarding dogs, you owe it not only to the people in your neighborhood, but also to other dog owners, to teach your dog to do its business only where this is allowed. It is not difficult for you or a problem for your dog; on the contrary!

You first go to a dog-walking area or a doggy toilet, where the dog can do its business, and then you take it for a nice walk, without having to worry about anything still to come. A precondition for this is, however, that you leave the house in time, but that is obvious. Do not take this command as seriously as the commands "Sit" and Stay." If it does not have the urge, your dog cannot produce anything on command; that is logical. The word that you are going to use from then on for defecating on command will be more of a friendly request. You teach your puppy this request by saying the word that you use for this every time your dog does its business. What sort of word this is does not matter, as long as it is always the same and clearly differs in sound from other commands. Always follow up with a friendly and approving "Good boy" (or "girl"). You do not have to repeat it ten times. Once is enough, although

*The indoor
kennel is an
indispensable help
in house-training*

you could possibly repeat it if you have the impression that
your dog has not heard you. In the beginning, say the word
whenever your dog relieves itself on its own initiative. Later,
take it to a dog-walking area and say it at the moment your dog
is sniffing around, while you reward it if it really does something. After some time, your dog will itself make the connec-
tion between the request and its deed, so that it is enough for
you in future to say the word at the dog-walking area.

Submission puddles
There are a number of forms of not being house-trained
which have nothing to do with unclean behavior. One of these
forms is the submissive puddle. You grumble at your dog; it
turns over onto its back or tries to make itself small (adopts a
submissive attitude) and wets itself. Whatever you do, never
punish your dog for this! Wetting itself, in combination with a
submissive attitude, is the most extreme manner in which a
pup can demonstrate its subordinate position. In the wild, a
wolf would never attack another wolf which displayed this
behavior. It curbs aggression. Ignore this type of urination. If
your dog does it often, then take a critical look at your contact
with the dog. This sort of behavior often presents in dogs that
are naturally submissive and unfortunately are being handled

in a manner which is inconsistent, unclear, and sometimes too severe.

Joyful puddles
Another form of "unclean" behavior, which actually has nothing to do with not being house-trained, is the puddle for joy. You come home and your dog jumps up at you, full of enthusiasm and wagging its tail, while at the same time losing a few drops of urine. Assuming that you have not left your dog alone for too long, during which time its bladder has become too full, it is usually young dogs that cannot control their bladders at times of great emotion. You should not punish your dog for this either, because it has absolutely no control over this. It is better to ignore your puppy completely—to limit the emotion—or call it outside and greet it out there where it can do no harm. By far the most dogs grow out of this in time, if not too much fuss is made about it.

Problems with being left alone
Loneliness is an unnatural situation for a dog. Many dogs learn how to handle this, but some have a lot of problems with it. These problems can manifest themselves in things like forgetting their house training, destructive behavior, and making a

Being alone is unnatural for a dog

noise while you are away. A combination of all three of these often occurs. It usually points to great frustration and fear: your dog is afraid to be alone. This behavior often occurs in dogs which were kept too long with their mothers. During their entire socialization phase they had the company of their mothers and brothers and sisters and they have never experienced being alone. The moment you close the door behind you they are overcome by panic. In some cases this speeds up the digestion, which results in diarrhea.

It is very difficult to get these dogs back on track, because they themselves can do little about it. Sometimes it can be helpful to build up their periods alone gradually. In the beginning, you leave the dog alone for just one or two minutes at the most and gradually you increase this period of time. Another, drastic measure is to get a second dog, so that your dog is never alone. Unfortunately, this does not always work. Sometimes an indoor kennel helps, not in the first place because a dog does not foul its own nest—if it gets very upset the dog simply can-

Havanese

Welsh Springer Spaniels

Cairn Terrier

not retain its urine and feces—but more so because the indoor kennel gives it a safe and comforting feeling. Some dogs grow out of this after a while, but there are also dogs that continue to give problems on this score.

Secret puddles

You walk for hours with your dog and it does nothing. You come home and later on notice that your dog has relieved itself somewhere behind the sofa or some other secret place. Your dog has learned not to relieve itself while people are looking. The reason for this is that during house training it was caught "in the act" and was punished. This has given the dog the idea that you do not approve of it relieving itself in your sight. To break through this pattern you will need to take your time. During the renewed house training the dog must never be left indoors unsupervized. It is best to put it in an indoor kennel and go out very regularly for walks, with the dog on a leash. Your dog then has no choice and has to do its job outside. It goes without saying that you then praise it with great enthusiasm. It may take some time before the dog gets used to this, but with a lot of time and effort most dogs can be convinced in the end.

7   BASIC TRAINING

Getting used to a collar

Before you can begin the basic training, your pup first has to get used to wearing a collar and being on a leash. Dogs generally become accustomed to this quite quickly. In the first instance, buy a soft collar—one made of woven nylon or soft leather, for example. Do not buy a collar for the dog to grow into, but buy one that fits. Put it on for an hour at first and

Start early with getting your pup used to wearing a collar

gradually increase the time. It is a great help to put the collar on just before you take the puppy out or, if your dog is sensitive to this, just before you give it its food. Your puppy is then so busy with eating or playing that it will forget the collar.

Nylon collar

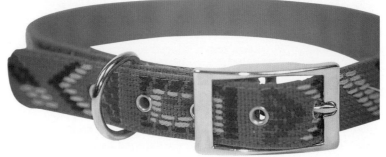

Right: English Bulldog pup

Teaching the puppy to walk on a leash

Once your dog has got used to its collar, you can fasten this to a leash. Do not pick up the leash yet, but allow your puppy to walk around with it, so that it can get used to this. When it is acclimatized, take the puppy outside and encourage it to walk with you. Do not pull on the leash, but coax your dog with kind words or a tasty tidbit. Some puppies react very strongly when they notice that their freedom is being restricted and they keep trying to struggle free. Praise the dog lavishly when it does not resist.

Beginning to teach commands
Precautionary measures

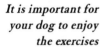

It is important for your dog to enjoy the exercises

In addition to the important basic rules discussed in Chapter 4, there are a number of things which must be taken into account during training.

Always train in places where your dog will be disturbed as little as possible

🦴 Keep your puppy motivated. A motivated pup not only learns faster but it continues to enjoy training, which is very important. To prevent your puppy from becoming demotivated, never go on too long with the training. In the beginning, five or ten minutes is long enough. Ring the changes by playing with your dog in between some of the commands. Never tire it by continually giving the same commands, because this makes the puppy bored and obstinate. Always give the commands clearly and in a fairly high (= friendly) tone.

➡ Prevent distraction. Young pups are very easily distracted. During training, too, it can happen that something else attracts your puppy's attention so that your commands are not getting registered properly. Train, therefore, in a quiet spot where few dogs come, and your dog will not be distracted by traffic or other people. If you have a large garden, then this is the ideal place. Do not allow others to watch or to interfere. Only one member of the family should take the training upon himself/herself and this person should continue to train the puppy until it knows all the commands. Only give a command when you know for sure that your puppy is not being distracted.

➡ Do not repeat yourself unnecessarily. Some people keep on repeating the same command. Before the dog gets a chance to "Sit," it has been told to do it six times already. From this, your dog will learn that you are prepared to give it a command several times. The words then lose their meaning. Attract your dog first by calling its name and, once you are sure you have its undivided attention, give the command loudly and clearly. It may be necessary to repeat a command once but do not go on doing this, as the command will lose its meaning for the pup.

Do not expect too much from your young pup

- Take it easy. Do not go out to train if you are in a bad mood. In this state of mind, you will not be able to tolerate as much from your dog, and you will correct it sooner or more severely than is necessary. Always remain quiet, and be fair; do not yell at your dog, and stay calm at all times.

- Do not demand too much. Young puppies are easily distracted. Certainly in the first phase they will only sit or lie for a moment. That does not matter. In the first instance, it is more than enough that your dog learns what the commands mean. Therefore, always praise the dog when it carries out your command, even though it jumps up again joyfully half a second later. Not until it knows the commands well can you expect more from your dog. Do not make the mistake of trying to teach the dog too much at once. If it is a "turbo-charged" pupil and learns what the command "Sit" means in one session, make that enough for one day. You can always see the next day whether it has remembered the command and then go on to the next exercise.

- Choose the right moment. A pup is less motivated with a full stomach than an empty one, although real hunger is not conducive to performance. Sleepy dogs or those that have yet to wake up properly are not the best pupils either. Finally, it is difficult for a puppy to keep its mind

Tasty morsels are an extra stimulus

on a lesson when it has a full bladder. You should therefore carefully choose the time you train your dog and
see to it that it has relieved itself beforehand.

Rewarding with food

Not all trainers agree as to whether you should teach new commands to your puppy with the aid of tasty tidbits. The under-
lying thought is that your dog then obeys for the food and not
because it wants to obey you. My opinion is that the dog listens
to you because this results in something positive. Whether that

*As long as your
pup does not obey
the command
"Here" properly,
keep it on the leash
during your daily
outings*

good feeling comes from a hug or a dog biscuit does not really matter. However, a dog biscuit or a piece of cheese cannot
take the place of contact with you. In addition to the tasty
morsel, a cuddle or a friendly word is also necessary. You can
phase out the giving of tidbits during training without any
problem as soon as your dog knows the commands.
Not all dog sweets and biscuits are suitable for training sessions, however. Biscuits that require a lot of chewing by your
dog are not very convenient, nor are large treats. Small pieces
of brown bread, either fresh or dried, pieces of cheese, dog biscuits, and small doggie sweets are, however, very suitable.

"Here" on command

At your command "Here," your pup must come to you directly, without hesitation or detours. Let your dog sniff about on a long leash until you are sure that its attention is elsewhere. Then call its name, followed by the friendly, but clearly spoken, command "Here!" If you squat down yourself, the dog will run up to you more quickly. If your puppy reacts to this command, reward it with a well-meant hug and, if it enjoys this, something tasty. If it does not react at all, repeat the command and give a short jerk on the leash. The intention is to make the dog uncomfortable if it does not obey your command (the leash is being jerked) and to make it pleasant for the dog when it obeys, because it can then expect a hug, kind words, and something tasty.

In general, the command "Here" should not give any problems. When your dog has mastered this, you can try it without a leash. Of course you will only do exercises off the leash in places where your dog cannot run away. If your dog is at the age of puberty, it may be more obstinate and do what it feels like doing. If it ignores your clearly spoken command of "Here" and you are sure that it has heard you, you can correct the dog by throwing something (at the dog!). The sudden fright it receives, followed by an inviting "Here," which you say while squatting a short distance from the pup, will surely bring the desired result.

Making mistakes while coming "Here"

Some dogs are very self-willed and do not listen directly to the command "Here," especially when they have passed the puppy stage. They make a game of it. Never let yourself be led into a game of this kind, because you will always be the loser. Never walk behind your dog to catch it, therefore, since this has the contrary effect and your dog will always be faster than you. You will get quicker and more lasting results if you squat down, or ignore the dog and walk away in the opposite direction. Ten to one the dog will suddenly run to you at speed. Remember, too, that your dog is always "Good" when it has obeyed your command. So it is also "Good" when it only returns after letting off steam for ten minutes.

Punishment is always associated with what the dog is doing at that moment. If you punish it for obeying a command, your dog will remember this the next time and will stay hovering around at a safe distance.

The left side
During "Heel," but during other exercises as well, your dog should be kept at your left side. This position originates from the world of the police dog. Weapons are usually worn on the

If you use gentle force with your hand, your dog will soon understand what you want from it

For lying down on command, say "Down"

Only give your dog the command "Stay" if you can check up on it

right side and, if the police dog walks on the left side of its owner, it does not hinder the owner from drawing their weapon. In today's dog training, even though it is not being trained for police or military purposes, the dog is always kept on the left side. In principle, of course, it does not matter whether it learns to walk on your left side or your right, but in view of the fact that left is compulsory for almost all canine sports, it is better to teach your dog this from the outset. You may possibly be involved in canine sports later and it will not be so easy to change your dog's habit then.

"Sit" on command

To teach your dog to sit on command, kneel down beside it. Say the name of the dog to attract its attention and then give the command "Sit." At the same time, push the hindquarters of your pup down gently with one hand, while supporting the forequarters with your other hand. You then maneuver it naturally into a sitting position.

If your pup sits, even for a second, praise it lavishly. If your pup tries to struggle free, try it again and keep on trying until you succeed. Here, too, the intention is that not obeying your command induces an uncomfortable feeling in your dog and obeying leads to clear approval, which makes the dog feel good.

Some pups love tasty treats. Sometimes you do not even have to exert pressure. By holding a biscuit in front of their nose, they sit down of their own accord. It goes without saying that, when your dog does sit down, you give it the biscuit immediately. Which of the two methods you apply depends on the character of your pup. At first, it is enough if your pup sits just for a moment. Later, when it is a bit older and knows the command well, you can expect the dog to continue to sit until you cancel the command. You can use the word "Okay" or something similar for this.

"Down" on command
You can teach your dog to lie down ("Down") as soon as it has learned the command "Sit" properly. For this, let the dog "Sit" and then give the command "Down." Then gently pull the dog's front paws forward to maneuver it into a lying position. Your other hand rests on the dog's hindquarters to prevent it from crawling away backward. At the same time, give the command "Down." If the dog stays down, reward it immediately. To teach this command to a dominant dog will require some doing, because this brings it into a subordinate position. Whatever happens, avoid a struggle, but do not give in too easily.

Young German Pointer

Right: Vizsla pup

Dogs that appreciate food can be taught this command in a different way. You hold a tasty morsel in your firmly clenched fist in front of its nose. Your dog cannot see the food, but it can smell it. First, tell the dog to "Sit" and then give the command "Down." Push it down gently with your other hand to indicate what you want. You can encourage your puppy, but remember that it is not "Good" until it is lying down. The lower the dog goes the more your hand opens. Once the dog is really lying down, you open your hand completely and it can eat the tidbit. At first, it is enough when your dog lies down just for a moment; later, you can require it to stay lying down until you give it the "Okay."

"Stay" on command

Staying on command implies that your dog has to stay exactly in the place where it is when you give the command. Basically, the dog can be lying down, sitting, or standing, but in the beginning it is easier to learn this from a sitting or lying position. Have your dog sit at your left side and put it on the leash. Ensure that you have your pup's undivided attention and give it the command "Stay." You can then take a step forward or sideways, but keep the dog on the leash. If the puppy remains

West Highland White Terriers

sitting, reward it at once. It is then a "Very good" dog. If it gets up at once— and most of them do—say "No!" and position it at exactly the same place again, after which you repeat the command and step away again. Some dogs are very stubborn, so keep on trying and do not give up too soon.

"Stay" is stay

Teach your dog to sit down first at every curb

Later, you can practice this command off the leash. Do it in a quiet, green area though, where the dog cannot just walk away, and only after it properly obeys the command "Here." Take note, however, that your dog must not discontinue a

command of its own accord. So always give "OK" at the end of the exercise. How soon you give the OK depends on the dog's capabilities and age but, as a rule, young pups are easily distracted and you cannot expect them to remain lying down for more than a couple of seconds before they get up again. Avoid this by giving the dog "OK," or "Alright," or whatever word you are going to use, fairly soon.

Some dogs have a tendency to "cheat." They creep toward you or walk on a bit and then lie down or sit again. Be consistent about not accepting this.

Waiting

You must not confuse the command "Wait" with "Stay."

"Wait" is used at a curb, when going outside with your dog, or getting in and out of the car. It is not too difficult to teach this, although very enterprising or bold pups will have more difficulty with it. Put a slip collar and leash on the dog. Take it to the front door, give the command "Wait," and then open the door. If the dog wants to go out, give a short jerk on the leash and say "Wait." It is not necessary for your pup to stay in the same basic position, as long as it stays behind the threshold. After a couple of seconds, you can end the waiting by rewarding the puppy and then saying "OK." See to it that you go through the door first; your dog always goes last.

"Heel" on command

On the command "Heel," your dog must walk next to you on your left. When you make a turn, the dog should follow you faultlessly, which also applies for changes of speed. Your dog can only do this when it keeps a sharp eye on you. It requires great concentration from your dog and good contact is therefore vital when doing this exercise. During the walk to heel, your dog will have to look up at you to keep contact. The intention is not that you adjust your movements or speed to the dog's, but vice versa. If you knock into your dog during walking, that is not your problem but the dog's: it should have paid more attention! That may sound rather unkind, but it is necessary for your dog to understand that you decide where the walk is leading to. In the wild, the leader of the pack takes no account of his subordinates—they follow him or get out of his way when he needs to pass. So wolves keep a sharp eye on their pack leader—although the leader scarcely notices them—and that is what you now expect from your pup. When it is not paying attention for a moment, you could bump into each other accidentally, but this does not matter a bit. It stimulates your pup into paying more attention. You should not, of course, comfort the dog if this happens!

Walking to heel in practice

During the walk, the leash should be slack

To teach walking to heel, always use a slip collar. Have the dog sitting on your left and hold the leash chest-high in front of you with both hands. Let the leash slacken a little. Say the dog's name, make sure you have its undivided attention, give the command "Heel" clearly, and walk forward in a straight line. If the dog holds back, coax it forward with something tasty,

and praise it if it walks nicely beside you. If it goes too far to the side, gets in your way, or pulls at the leash, give a short jerk on the leash. The intention is for your dog to walk exactly beside you, not in front of you and not a yard away. If your dog comes and walks nicely beside you, probably also looking up at you, then it is a particularly "Good dog" and you should tell it so. Looking up at you is a sign that the dog is trying to contact you and wants to do its best to walk to heel. Reward the pup for this during the walk with kind words. A small bag, filled with tasty morsels from which you give your dog a treat now and then when it is doing well, can work wonders if your dog appreciates this.

Wait until your dog has mastered walking to heel well before cutting down on the rewards. This exercise can be extended later to include right or left about turns, or turning to the left or right, and abrupt stops during which the dog has to sit. The leash should hang loosely, whatever your speed.

You can easily tell whether the dog understands and is enjoying this exercise by the way its tail is wagging and it is looking up happily at you.

Pulling at the leash

"Heel" is a real exercise, which must not be confused with teaching the dog not to pull on the leash. It is therefore not the intention that you have your dog continually "To heel" during your daily walks. If you give this command, you demand optimal concentration. Your pup cannot relax and sniff about here and there and thus cannot gather impressions. Pulling on the leash is punished by a short but clear jerk on the leash. You do not need to reward the dog when it does not pull. The non-occurrence of the jerk on the leash is enough of a reward and teaches the dog that pulling on the leash only produces negative results.

"Place"

The command "Place" is used when you want your dog to go to its basket or indoor kennel. For this, pick your puppy up and put it in its indoor kennel or basket. Say "Place" while you do this. If your dog stays in that place, even if only for a moment, praise it immediately ("That's good! That's your place!"). If it gets out of the basket immediately, put it back in again and repeat the command. When you have done this a number of times, your dog will understand what this word means and you will in future only have to give the command "Place," while perhaps pointing to the place to make yourself clear. The best time to practice this, of course, is when your pup has finished playing and is getting a bit tired. The dog is not allowed to leave its place until you have given the "OK," so do not send your puppy to its place if you cannot keep an eye on it.

Every dog can learn to roll over or lie on its side

Other exercises

In actual fact, all exercises that you want to teach your dog
come down to the same thing: give a clear command when you
have your dog's undivided attention, stimulate the dog to obey
the command by maneuvering it into the desired position, and
give encouragement when it is doing well. Subsequently, a
reward will come its way in the form of a hug, a kind word,
and a tasty tidbit if it obeys the command correctly. Make
obeying your commands as much fun for the pup as possible
and see to it that ignoring commands has negative associations
(a jerk on the leash). In this way, you can teach your dog to stand
still at the command of "Still," whereby you hold a tidbit in
front of its nose and support its belly with your other hand so it
cannot sit down, and say "On your side," implying that it must
lie on its side. This command is very useful if your dog needs a
lot of grooming. If you like, you can teach your puppy to sit up,
or walk on its back paws, or even roll over, just by being clear in
your commands and rewarding good behavior.

8 EXERCISE AND ACTIVITY

Walking

Dogs grow very fast, particularly the medium-sized and large breeds. Especially in the first year, this growth makes extra heavy demands on the bones, joints, and tendons. If the loco-motor apparatus is overloaded or wrongly used, defects can occur that will cause lifelong problems. This overloading occurs if a dog climbs stairs every day, makes too many jumps or twisting movements, plays roughly with other dogs, or goes on exhausting walks. Slipping on a polished floor indoors has also done irreparable damage to many young dogs.

Some young dogs are so enthusiastic and full of energy that they do not know when to stop, although their bodies cannot take any more.

Fast growth requires a lot of energy

Turning movements such as this are very bad during the growth phase

This German Shepherd Dog obviously gets great pleasure out of retrieving

Spare your puppy these things, but do not be too careful. Their muscles must have the opportunity to develop well and this will certainly not happen if you wrap your dog in cotton batting. Give it a chance to develop its muscles in a healthy manner by letting it make chiefly straight, running movements and taking it out for several short walks a day. You cannot prevent it larking and racing about from time to time, but do not overreact. Later on, when your dog has built up a healthy constitution through good care in its first year, you can walk for hours in the woods and over fields.

Scents during its daily walk

You will notice that, during your daily walks, your dog will use its nose a lot. When it sniffs at street corners, poles, and bushes, appearing to be extremely interested in these scents—it is really interested. Your dog has an excellent sense of smell and what it smells during these outings constitutes an excellent source of information. One of the things your dog smells is the urine traces of other dogs. From these, it can distinguish whether the sender is high or low in rank and whether there is a bitch in season. Has a new dog come to live in the neighborhood or has one just left? The presence of a new scent or the absence of a familiar scent marker will tell your dogs these things. Males do this more than bitches. They plant their scent

Right: Scents play an important role in the mutual communication between dogs

markers at set places and dominant males also cover other dogs' scents with their own urine. Feces have the same sort of function. The anal gland gives off a unique odor which is added to the feces heap. Because scents are an important part of the communication between dogs, it is not very kind of you to forbid your dog to set out a scent marker or to have a good sniff at certain places from time to time. Just as we read the newspaper, so a dog sniffs up information. During training sessions, however, its attention must be fully devoted to you and, when you have given a command, the dog must never let itself be distracted.

Sometimes you have to forbid a male from putting out a scent marker. Not everyone appreciates their garden fence or conifer being the "talking point" for all the dogs in the neighborhood.

You must never accept chasing after cats and cattle or challenging stares toward other dogs in the street

Right: Sloughi pup

Chasing cats and other animals

Some dogs have more hunting instinct than others. You will probably have noticed that during your dog's socialization period. One puppy reacts with great interest to sheep and cats, while another does not even notice them. You will realize that those dogs with a strongly developed innate hunting instinct are likely to cause problems later by chasing cattle and other animals. Cats and cattle in particular are seldom unmoved if a dog runs up to them barking. They run away and this just strengthens the hunting instinct. Remember that, once a dog has learned what fun it can be to chase after prey, it will be very difficult to prevent this behavior later. It is not, therefore, funny, and certainly nothing to be proud of, if your dog frightens the life out of a possibly much larger cat by angry growling and barking. Put a stop to this undesired behavior at once, to prevent your dog from making a habit of it. Once it has become an adult, you will have a dog with a problem. If your dog makes a move, for example by barking, or stands fixated and ready to spurt off after its "prey," you must punish this immediately with a short, sharp jerk on the slip collar, at the same time saying in a low, angry voice "Bad dog." Do not wait until it is halfway there, but correct your dog immediately. If your dog is rather headstrong, take it regularly to places where

there are cats or cattle and make this a part of the total education and training program, until the dog has lost interest in other animals.

In the car

Your dog will regularly be transported in the car. Not every dog enjoys car trips. There are various reasons for this. If you only take your dog in the car to visit the vet, then it will associate the car with something negative and will become more and more difficult to get into the car. Take your dog from the outset on regular short trips and see to it that both riding and the final destination are positive experiences. The puppy then connects riding in the car with, for example, a lovely walk in the woods and will be happy to go with you.

Some dogs get car-sick. This can partly be overcome by not giving any food beforehand. If the dog continues to be troubled by this, you can get medication from the vet for it. If it is a long trip, stop regularly and give the dog a chance to stretch its legs and relieve itself.

Irritating behavior during the car trip

Some dogs behave in an irritating manner during a car trip. It is normal for your dog to whine a little or bark from excitement sometimes. It knows that something nice is going to happen. It is a different matter if your dog continuously barks and whines or jumps up and down on the back seat. This behavior must be stopped as soon as possible. This takes time and effort but this is nothing compared with the irritation that your dog will stir up in you during car trips—if you take your dog along with you, because these dogs are, more often than not, left at home. Cure your dog of this behavior as soon as possible by correcting it with the slip collar. There must of course be two of you for this, since drivers have to keep their minds on the road. By breaking through this behavior as resolutely and quickly as possible, you will prevent it from becoming a habit.

Safety during car trips

Many dogs travel loose on the back seat of the car, but this is not a safe manner of transport. It is better to put an indoor kennel in the car for a dog. This can be the same indoor kennel that you use in the house, but could also be one that you always keep in the car. When your dog gets used to this, it will enjoy being in the kennel because that is its safe, familiar bed.

A dog trailer

In station wagons, you can fit a metal dog rack between the passenger seats and the storage space, which will prevent your dog from being thrown through the whole car during an abrupt stop or a swerve. Some people prefer a special dog trailer. The disadvantage of these is that they are rather pricey, you have to adjust your speed, and your dog is not so well protected in a collision. The advantage is that your car stays clean.

Cycling

Walking alongside your bicycle, especially trotting, whereby your dog moves its left hind leg and right front leg (and vice versa) at the same time, is ideal physical exercise. The movements are in a straight line and your dog gets optimal use of its muscles, which promotes muscular development. This is frequently done in some parts of the world but in some areas it is not allowed if the dog is on the leash, since this would restrict your control of the bike. Where it is possible to let the dog run off the leash behind the bicycle, it should be no problem. It is often said that a dog must not walk beside a bicycle before its first birthday, but this is only partly true. If you only cycle for short distances and adjust your speed to that of the dog, you can begin with this when the dog is six months old. Always adjust your speed to suit the dog and prevent it from becoming tired. Gradually build up the cycle trips and, along with this, the condition of your dog. An athlete would not be able to run a marathon straight after the winter break without getting injured, and the same applies for your dog. For reasons of safety, teach your dog right from the beginning that it must always run on the curb side of the bicycle. It goes without saying that, before you start to cycle with your dog, it must be well socialized and perfectly under (voice) control. If it suddenly lunges out at another dog or jumps to one side because it is frightened by something, both you and the dog will be endangered, as well as other road users.

Many bicycle trips are on asphalt roads. Remember that asphalt can get very hot in the summer, painfully damaging your dog's pads, and it will take a long time for such an injury to heal. In addition to this, a dog has the tendency to go on, even when it really cannot. The combination of over exertion and heat is not good for any dog, but for Huskies and some Mastiffs can cause acute and dangerous conditions. Therefore, cycle only in moderate temperatures, and only in the mornings and evenings at the height of the summer.

Not all dogs like water

Swimming and retrieving are an ideal combination in hot weather

This Swedish Vallhund enjoys retrieving

Swimming

On hot, summer days, swimming is ideal exercise. The dog uses all its muscles and is not likely to injure itself in the water. Many dogs love water by nature and can hardly pass alongside a pool or lake without taking a dip. Other dogs need a bit more encouragement. You can teach your dog to swim by going into the water with it and supporting it under the breast and belly when it has no contact with the ground. If your dog loves to retrieve, you can throw a retrieving block into the water, throwing it a bit further every time, so that it gradually acclimatizes. Never just push the dog into the water. This Spartan method only encourages fear of water and will also cause your dog to have less confidence in you. Water which is unsafe for humans because of dangerous bacteria, or because there are unpredictable undercurrents, is also unsafe for dogs. Only allow your dog to swim in safe places. It can become entangled in fishing nets and trailing water plants, so be careful with your dog in those areas. Finally, ensure that it can get out of the water without too much difficulty; steeply sloping banks can be impossible to climb for many dogs.

Retrieving blocks

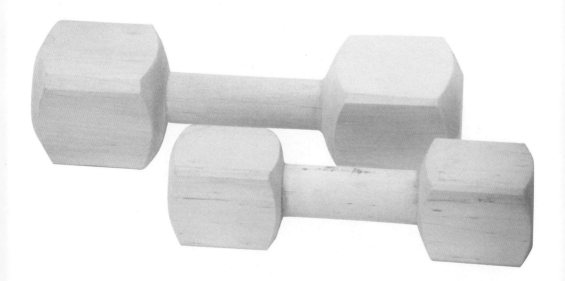

Games

Retrieving

Retrieving is a game enjoyed by most dogs. Hunting dogs and sheep-dogs in particular love to do it, but many terriers also love to chase after a stick or a ball and bring it back to the boss. You can start early with teaching this to your puppy by calling it whenever it has something in its mouth, followed by the friendly command "Fetch!" If the dog comes to you with its toy, praise it and exchange the toy for a small biscuit before throwing the toy again. You can perfect this later, but in the beginning it is enough just to stimulate retrieving. If your dog is holding something in its mouth which you would prefer it

Only play this kind of tug-of-war game if you can win

not to have, such as a shoe, let the animal retrieve it and then throw something that is allowed. For retrieving, it is better to use a toy or a special retrieving block instead of a stick or a branch. These can have sharp points and there is a real danger of an enthusiastic retriever being injured through them.

Tug-of-war

Tug-of-war is a game that many dogs enjoy. For this, your dog pulls on one end of a thick rope or strong toy and you pull on the other. This sort of game is not entirely without risk, however. Your dog will not necessarily see it as a game. The dog can be deadly serious and turn it into a power struggle. If it wins the game, it will give the dog the idea that it is stronger than you and, if you have a dominant pup, this can certainly lead to problems later. If you are in any doubt as to whether you can continue to win the game when your dog is an adult, it is better not to start it. If, on the other hand, you have a pup which could do with some more confidence, it is good to let it win more often. The dog will not really challenge your position, but will gain self-confidence. After finishing the game, put the rope or toy away and do not give it to the dog.

Tracking games

A tug-of-war can turn into a power struggle

Tracking games are great fun for most dogs. For example, you can hide a favorite ball under a bucket and let the dog look for it. Later, you can make it more and more difficult by hiding different balls amongst which your pup has to find its "own"

ball. Another good and exciting game for a dog with a feeling for detection and a good nose for sniffing things out is played with pieces of cloth hung on a low clothesline, from which your dog has to find one piece of cloth that you have had in your pocket for a while. You should allow the dog to search independently and without help, but praise it lavishly when it has found the right ball or piece of cloth.

Bordeaux Mastiff puppy